JAMESTOWN EDUCATION

THE CONTEMPORARY READER

VOLUME 2, NUMBER 5

Mc
Graw
Hill
Glencoe
McGraw-Hill

New York, New York   Columbus, Ohio   Chicago, Illinois   Peoria, Illinois   Woodland Hills, California

Glencoe/McGraw-Hill

A Division of The **McGraw·Hill** Companies

ISBN: 0-89061-830-5

© 1998 by the McGraw-Hill Companies, Inc. All rights
reserved. Except as permitted under the United States Copyright Act,
no part of this publication may be reproduced or distributed in any
form or by any means, or stored in a database or retrieval system,
without prior permission of the publisher.

Send all inquiries to:
Glencoe/McGraw-Hill
8787 Orion Place
Columbus, OH 43240-4027

Printed in the United States of America

7 8 9 10 11 12 026 08 07 06 05 04 03

CONTENTS

Pronunciation Key

ă	mat	o͞o	food
ā	date	o͝o	look
â	bare	ŭ	drum
ä	father	yo͞o	cute
ĕ	wet	û	fur
ē	see	*th*	then
ĭ	tip	th	thin
ī	ice	hw	which
î	pierce	zh	usual
ŏ	hot	ə	alone
ō	no		open
ô	law		pencil
oi	boil		lemon
ou	loud		campus

The handsome S.S. *Edmund Fitzgerald* was once known for setting many cargo records over the years. Today the ship is best remembered for the tragic and violent way it met its end.

DOOMED

To Disaster

*What caused the 1975 shipwreck
on Lake Superior?*

1   It was a beautiful day—almost picture-perfect.
The sky was bright and the wind was low. The
29 crew members of the S.S. *Edmund Fitzgerald*
[fĭts jĕr´ əld] looked forward to a pleasant jour-
ney. They had made the trip across Lake Superior
many times before. Unfortunately, this time would
be different. This trip would end in disaster.

Weather Warning

2   The *Edmund Fitzgerald* was built in 1958. At the
time, it was the biggest ship ever to sail on the
Great Lakes. It measured 729 feet long. For 17
years, the ship had made many trips across these
lakes. On November 9, 1975, it set out again, carry-
ing thousands of tons of iron ore. The crew
loaded the ore in Superior, Wisconsin. They
planned to take it to Detroit, Michigan, for use
in steel mills.

3   The ship set out at 4:30 P.M. That night, the crew received a weather update on the radio. A storm was headed their way, and a gale[1] warning had been issued.

4   Captain Ernest McSorley, however, was not too worried. The *Edmund Fitzgerald* had seen its share of storms. One benefit of sailing the Great Lakes was that the trips were short. Land was never far off. Even during bad storms, the *Fitzgerald* had always been able to make it to safety by "running for it."

5   Even so, McSorley took proper notice of the warning. He talked to the captain of a nearby ship, the S.S. *Arthur M. Anderson.* Just 15 miles from the *Fitzgerald,* the *Anderson* was crossing Lake Superior as well.

6   The two captains agreed that they should change course. They would both steer their ships farther north, near the Canadian shore. It would be a longer route than usual, but a safer one. Using it, the ships would gain more shelter from the storm.

The Witch of November

7   By the morning of November 10, the storm had moved in. The *Fitzgerald's* crew knew they would have a rough ride ahead. November

---

[1] gale: a wind with a speed of 32 to 63 miles per hour

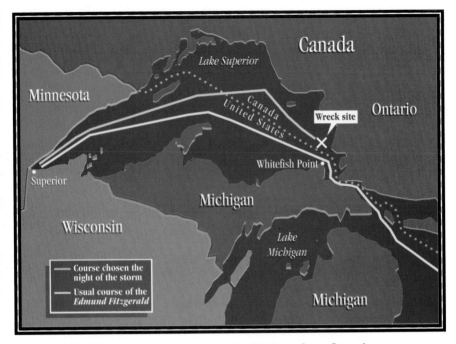

The *Fitzgerald* set out for Detroit, Michigan, from Superior, Wisconsin, on its usual course. Because of the storm, the ship changed to a more sheltered route farther north.

storms tended to be nasty. A bad one was called a "Witch of November." And this witch did look mean. A heavy rain was falling. The wind was gusting up to 60 miles per hour, and the waves were already 10 feet high.

8   By 3:00 P.M., the *Fitzgerald* was near the Canadian shore. By then, the ship had begun to list, or tilt. Such listing meant that the ship was taking on water.

Some life preservers, a life raft, and a few oars were all that was recovered from the *Edmund Fitzgerald*. The ship fell victim to a fierce "Witch of November" without one signal for help.

9 No one on board was really surprised. Again and again, high waves splashed over the deck. McSorley and his crew figured that this topside water was causing the list. The crew started up two of the ship's pumps to get rid of the water.

10 Meanwhile, the rain had turned to snow. The *Anderson* was still just 16 miles behind the *Fitzgerald*. But with the wind and snow, it became impossible for the two crews to see each other.

The Storm Grows Worse

11 By 4:00 P.M., the wind had gotten even stronger. The gusts now reached 100 miles per hour. The waves rose 15 feet or higher.

12 For the men on board the *Fitzgerald,* things were going from bad to worse. The storm knocked out the radar antennas of both ships. Then a nearby lighthouse lost its light and its beacon.[2] Now the crew had no way to tell where the shore was. McSorley put in a radio call to the *Anderson.* He asked for help in tracking the *Fitzgerald's* course.

13 By 6:40 P.M., the waves had reached frightening heights. Some were close to 25 feet tall. In a radio call to the *Anderson,* McSorley said it was one of the worst storms he had ever seen. From a man who had sailed the Great Lakes for more than 40 years, it was a strong statement.

Last Words

14 At 7:00 P.M., McSorley called the *Anderson* again to say that he was slowing down his ship. That way, the *Anderson* could pull closer to the *Fitzgerald.* Before the call ended at 7:10 P.M., McSorley was asked if the *Fitzgerald* was still listing: "By the way, how are you making out with your problems?" asked the *Anderson's* first mate.

---

[2]beacon: a radio that sends out a warning or guiding signal

15   "We are holding our own," McSorley answered. No one knew it at the time, but those would be his last words to the world.

Disaster Strikes

16   A few minutes later, the snow stopped. The crew aboard the *Anderson* thought they might be able to see the lights of the *Fitzgerald* once again. Looking out across the water, they *did* see lights. But the lights came from other ships—ships much farther away than the Fitzgerald could be.

17   By 7:20 P.M., the *Anderson's* crew saw that the *Fitzgerald* was no longer on their radar screen. They tried to call the ship but got no answer. The *Fitzgerald* had disappeared. The U.S. Coast Guard and other ships in the area tried to find the *Fitzgerald* and its crew. After four days, searchers with special equipment found the missing ship. It lay on the bottom of Lake Superior, 17 miles from where it was to dock. As for the crew, not one body was ever found or ever washed ashore from the wreck.

A Sudden End

18   No one could understand what had happened. The *Fitzgerald's* crew had issued no distress call. They had not launched any lifeboats or even put on life jackets. Clearly, the ship must have gone down suddenly, in a matter of seconds. But how? And why?

Bearing the names of the 29 crew members, this copy of the ship's bell was placed on the *Edmund Fitzgerald*, 550 feet below Lake Superior.

19   No one is sure what happened on that fateful night. It seems likely that the cargo area became flooded with water. A wave could have pitched the ship's bow[3] [bou] down below the surface. With the extra weight of the water trapped on board, the ship would not have been able to right[4] itself. The heavy iron ore might then have shifted forward, plunging the ship to the bottom of the lake.

---

[3] bow: the front section of a ship
[4] right: to return to an upright or vertical position

Still a Mystery

20   That explanation still leaves a big question unanswered. How did water get into the cargo area? The Coast Guard said the ship's hatch[5] covers might have come loose. But others disagree. They point out that there were more than 1,000 cover latches on the ship. The crew would have fastened all latches when the ship left port. They would surely have rechecked these latches upon word of the gale warning. So if one cover latch was loose, some people think, they should *all* have been loose—and they were not. A seasoned[6] crew like the one on the *Fitzgerald* would not have been so careless.

21   Some say the ship strayed into shallow water. If it scraped bottom, the ship's hull[7] might have been damaged. The damage could have caused a sudden flood of water into the cargo area. But a later check by divers revealed no damage to the ship's bottom.

22   And so the mystery remains. To this day, even after later searches, no one is sure what caused the wreck of the *Edmund Fitzgerald* and its crew of 29 men.

---

[5] hatch: an opening in the deck of a ship
[6] seasoned: experienced and ready to do a job well
[7] hull: the frame or body of a ship

In Memory

23   The night the *Fitzgerald* was lost, families of the crew waited for their loved ones to come home. But none of the crew ever came home. The families suffered many years of pain and sorrow. In 1995, a special work team went to Lake Superior. Workers cut away the bell from the ruins of the *Fitzgerald,* 550 feet below the lake. The bell was presented to the relatives of the crew. It was rung 30 times, once for each crew member and a last time for all who have lost their lives at sea. A copy of the bell, with the names of the 29 crew members on it, was placed on the ship. The ship's real bell now rests in the Shipwreck Museum at Whitefish Point, Michigan. It is the centerpiece of a memorial to the S.S. *Edmund Fitzgerald* and its crew. ◆

QUESTIONS

1. What did Captain McSorley do when he received the gale warning?
2. What is a "Witch of November"?
3. What problem did the *Fitzgerald* have during the afternoon of November 10?
4. How did the *Anderson* help out during the *Fitzgerald's* last hours?
5. What are two ideas about why the *Fitzgerald* sank?

The Art of Acupuncture

What is acupuncture?
Can it ease pain and cure disease?

1 For more than 2,000 years, the Chinese have used acupuncture [ăk′yo͞o pŭngk chər] to treat health problems. They use it to ease pain, treat arthritis, and cure other ailments. They even use it to treat deafness. The Chinese and other Asians still use acupuncture today.

2 Most Westerners[1] know little about acupuncture. Yet acupuncture is growing more and more popular in the United States. Doctors who research this ancient healing art want to find out how it works. They want to know *why* it works.

---

[1] Westerner: a person who lives in or near North America, South America, or Western Europe

An acupuncturist places thin needles in special spots in the skin of the ear to treat this woman's pain. The reasons for acupuncture's success are not fully understood.

An Ancient Art

3   Acupuncturists stick needles into a person's skin. They use very thin needles. Usually, they insert the needles just a fraction of an inch into the skin.

4   Acupuncturists carefully place each needle in a precise spot. There are more than 500 such spots, called *points,* on the human body. Acupuncturists place needles in different points, depending on the ailment they treat. For instance, they may insert needles in 40 different points. Or they may use only one point.

5   How does the practice work? First, experts insert the needles. Then they move the needles gently. In ancient days, they twirled the needles by hand. Some experts use this method today. Others heat up the needles. Still others send a weak electric current through the needles.

6   Acupuncturists say that the moving needles block pain. The needles, they claim, can control blood pressure and can help addicts withdraw from alcohol and drugs. They can also control appetite and relieve asthma [ăz´ mə].

Pain-Free Surgery

7   Western doctors are starting to believe that some of these claims have value. One study compared two groups of stroke[2] victims. The first group got

---

[2] stroke: a sudden weakness or loss of consciousness, feeling, or movement due to a lack of oxygen in the brain

regular therapy. The other group got regular therapy *plus* acupuncture. The second group made a faster and more complete recovery.

8 The Chinese point to even stronger proof. Chinese doctors often use acupuncture during surgery in place of anesthetics[3] [ăn ĭs thĕt´ ĭks]. Acupuncture, they say, works better than drugs. Patients stay alert—but

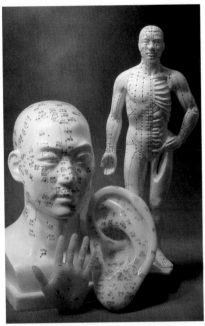

The Chinese have long believed that a strong life force, or *ch'i*, flows through the body along energy paths. On these paths are more than 500 acupuncture points.

pain free—during surgery. There are no side effects, and patients recover quickly. Acupuncture also costs much less than drugs.

9 In China, doctors use acupuncture for nearly one-third of all surgeries. They often use it for both minor and major operations. Doctors have used acupuncture for surgery on the heart, lungs, eyes, kidneys, and brain.

---

[3] anesthetic: a drug that causes one to lose feeling, especially the feeling of pain

10   There is a downside. On some people, acupuncture does not work. On others, the effect may wear off during long operations. Still other patients feel painful tugs or pulls.

11   Even so, acupuncture has gained much support in the United States. About 9,000 acupuncture professionals hold millions of sessions about the method each year. Some patients turn to these doctors when mainstream[4] treatment fails. Others believe that the body can be stirred to heal itself.

An Ancient Theory

12   How does acupuncture affect the body? How does it block pain? According to ancient Chinese theory, the human body contains a strong life force, or *ch'i* [chē]. This force controls the body's organs. It provides the energy that makes the body work. The energy travels through the body along set paths. Sometimes the energy flow is disrupted[5] and gets out of balance. This imbalance causes pain and disease.

13   To ease pain or cure disease, *ch'i* must be restored, and balance must be returned. Doctors who use acupuncture place needles at certain points along the energy paths. The needles stimulate the energy flow. The Chinese say that such movement restores *ch'i* and, in turn, the health of both body and mind.

---

[4] mainstream: usual or current
[5] disrupted: broken up

Western Theories

14 Many Western doctors agree that acupuncture eases pain. But they have different theories to explain why. One theory involves the body's natural painkillers. Doctors have found chemicals in the body that kill pain. Perhaps acupuncturists already knew the places in the body where the needles could trigger the natural painkillers.

15 A second theory has to do with how the brain senses pain. When a part of the body gets hurt, it sends a message to special pain receptors. These receptors, found in the brain and spinal cord, get a pain message. They send it on to tell the body that it feels pain. A person says "ouch!" only after the receptors send a pain message.

16 Some doctors think that acupuncture needles can turn off these pain receptors. They think that the

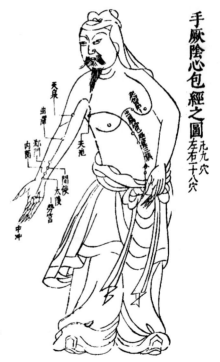

This early Chinese drawing from A.D. 1031 shows some of the many acupuncture points on the human body.

The ancient practice of making medicine from herbs is a popular alternative treatment.

needles cause a burst of messages. These messages flood the receptors and cause an overload. Because the receptors cannot send any pain messages, the patient feels no pain. When the needles are removed, the overload ends. The receptors can once again send pain messages.

Alternative Medicine

17 No one is sure why acupuncture works, but it has helped a large number of people. This treatment is part of a growing trend called alternative[6]

---

[6] alternative: being one choice among two or more choices

medicine. Alternative treatments use the body's ability to heal itself.

18   Alternative treatments vary widely. Prayer, music, and dance are some examples. Yoga, meditation, special breathing, herb therapy, and healing by touch are others.

19   Some alternative treatments are known as "folk" treatments. They seem old-fashioned, yet they often work. Today, many Western doctors use these treatments with their patients. Some people say that this is daring. But the Chinese probably say, "What took you so long?" ◆

QUESTIONS

1. What do supporters of acupuncture say that this treatment can do?
2. How is acupuncture performed?
3. What proof do Chinese doctors give to show that acupuncture works?
4. What role do the Chinese believe *ch'i* plays in a person's health?
5. What two theories do Western doctors give to explain why acupuncture works?

The Boston Marathon

*Why is the Boston Marathon such
a famous sporting event?*

1   Each year for over 100 years, runners have
gathered outside of Boston, Massachusetts. They
toe the starting line. They hear the starting gun,
jump into motion, and race to the finish line. It is
not an easy race. The finish line is in downtown
Boston, more than 26 miles away.

2   This yearly event is known as the Boston
Marathon. Runners from around the world
compete in the race. The Boston Marathon has
become a huge sporting event. Many runners feel
that it is the most important race of the year. To
them, the race is second only to the Olympics.

**Nearly 40,000 runners in the 100th Boston Marathon (1996)
filled the streets on their way to the start line.**

The First "Marathon"

3   The first "marathon" took place in ancient Greece. In 490 B.C., the Greeks won a battle at a town called Marathon. A Greek soldier carried the news to Athens. He ran all the way—about 25 miles.

4   In 1896, the modern Olympics were founded. The organizers chose to honor the ancient "marathon." They added a marathon race to the Olympics. The course was 25 miles long. In 1908, the distance was changed to 26 miles, 385 yards— the course length for all modern marathons.

Rain didn't stop Ellison "Tarzan" Brown from crossing the finish line in the 1939 Boston Marathon. A Native American, Brown also won the race in 1936.

The Boston Tradition

5 The first Boston Marathon took place on April 19, 1897. Fifteen runners lined up in a small town near Boston. They ran 25 miles into the city. Most of the course was dirt roads. There was no prize money, and few people came to watch.

6 This humble[1] event was the start of a great tradition. Today, the Boston Marathon is the oldest annual marathon. It has been called "the Super Bowl of foot racing." Nearly 40,000 men and women ran the race in 1996. About two million people lined the roads to watch. Now the roads of the course are paved. And Marathon winners earn prize money, fame, and glory.

By the 1970s, studies were showing that running improved a person's health. It works for this runner, who is still going strong at age 87.

The Running Craze

7 In the early years of the Boston Marathon, running was not a popular sport. Few runners took part in the race. They ran more slowly than today's winners. Their pace was more like a fast jog.

---

[1] humble: not grand or important

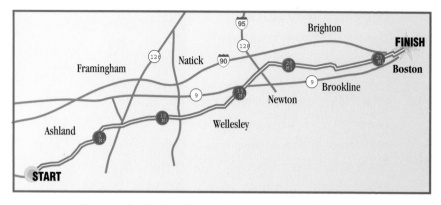

Runners in the first Boston Marathon ran a 25-mile course from Ashland, Massachusetts, to downtown Boston. In 1908, the starting line was moved to Hopkinton, changing the distance to 26.2 miles—the standard length for modern marathons.

8   Most people thought the runners were odd. Why did they want to run so far? Why put themselves through the pain?

9   In the 1960s, people's views about running started to change. Doctors began to prove that running can promote good health. People soon realized that running has many perks. It is great exercise, it is free, and it requires little equipment. It can be done just about anytime, anywhere. And just about anyone can run.

10   More and more people began to jog and run. Suddenly, running was a popular pastime. Some people ran just a few miles a week. Others began to run 50 miles or more per week. Still others began to wonder if they too could run in a marathon. More and more people signed up to run the Boston race.

11   By the 1970s, thousands entered the Boston Marathon each year. They came from every state and almost every country. In fact, too many people wanted to enter the race. The course could not hold them all. So the organizers made a rule. Runners now had to qualify to enter the race. They had to prove that they could run the distance within a set time. The time depended on a runner's sex and age. The new rule helped limit the large number of runners.

A Runner's View

12   In one way, the Boston Marathon is not a hard course. It starts in Hopkinton and ends in downtown Boston. Overall, the course is downhill. That is, the finish line is lower than the starting line.

Uta Pippig of Germany struggles up Heartbreak Hill in the 1997 Boston Marathon. Although she finished fourth, Pippig was the first to win the women's race three years in a row—in 1994, 1995, and 1996.

13   However, there are many ups and downs in between. The worst "up" comes at the 22-mile mark. At this point in the race, runners have just about run out of energy. They must finish the race on sheer

Cosmas Ndeti of Kenya, a country in Africa, set the record in the 1994 Marathon for the fastest running time ever. He finished all 26.2 hilly miles of the course in 2 hours, 7 minutes, 15 seconds.

will. This part of the course is known as "Heartbreak Hill." It is not just the large size and steep slope of the hill that make runners call it the place where they "hit the wall." It is also *where* Heartbreak Hill comes in the 26.2-mile course—toward the end—that makes some tired runners unable to climb it. Many runners have collapsed on this hill, ending their dream of finishing the race. Everyone agrees that "heartbreak" is the perfect name for this hill.

14   The race has other hazards[2] as well. The biggest one is the weather. April can be a cruel month in Boston. It is sometimes bone-chillingly cold, with a strong east wind blowing in runners' faces. Imagine running more than 26 miles *against* the wind.

15   On the other hand, the weather often turns hot and humid. This extreme can cause problems too. Some runners get cramps, get dizzy, or faint from the heat.

Some Great Winners

16   In the Boston Marathon, everyday people can run against world-class[3] runners. For most people, the goal is simply to finish the race. But for the world-class runners, the goal is to win.

17   Over the years, there have been some great winners of this famous race. One crowd pleaser was Johnny Kelley, who won the race twice. His second win was in 1945, when Kelley was 39 years old. Many people would have stopped running after that, but not Kelley. He ran in a total of 61 Boston Marathons. In fact, he kept running until he was in his eighties.

---

[2] hazard: a danger
[3] world-class: ranked as one of the best in the world

18   Bill Rodgers won the race four times. Three of these wins were in a row. Cosmas Ndeti [ən dě′ tē] of Kenya also won three times in a row. Ndeti set the course record in 1994. His running time was 2 hours, 7 minutes, 15 seconds.

19   The Boston Marathon was a male-only race until 1972. Since then, women have flocked to Boston to compete in the race. Women run alongside men, but they compete only against other women. Uta Pippig of Germany holds the best running time for women. In 1994, she ran the race in 2 hours, 21 minutes, 45 seconds.

20   Pippig was once asked why she ran in Boston. Her answer sums up the feeling of many runners. "It's the oldest race, it's the oldest marathon," she said. "You want to go to heaven and you want to go to Boston." ◆

Q UESTIONS

1. How did the first "marathon" get its name?
2. In what year did the first Boston Marathon take place?
3. How has the Boston Marathon changed over the years?
4. What are two hardships that runners face during the Boston Marathon?
5. Who are two big names in the history of the Boston Marathon?

President Bill Clinton signed the hotly-debated North American Free Trade Agreement (NAFTA) on December 8, 1993, in Washington, D.C.

NAFTA: Boon or Bust?

What does the North American Free Trade Agreement mean for the United States' economy?

1   **I**n 1993, Congress approved the North American Free Trade Agreement (NAFTA). The agreement went into effect on January 1, 1994. NAFTA was a hot topic then. And it has not cooled down much since. Some people love this trade pact, but others bitterly oppose it. Why has NAFTA stirred up so much trouble?

What is NAFTA?

2   NAFTA is a kind of treaty—a written agreement between nations. It was signed by the United States, Canada, and Mexico. The goal of NAFTA was to make trade between these countries free. Free trade would lead to more trade and, therefore, benefit all three nations.

3   The three countries have always traded, or exchanged goods and services, with each other.

This map depicts the flow of North American trade.

But they all had barriers to free trade, mostly as import taxes, or tariffs.[1] Most of the tariffs were between the United States and Mexico. For example, a U.S. tariff on clothing made in Mexico added to the cost of Mexican-made clothing sold in the United States. So clothing made in Mexico was no cheaper for Americans to buy than U.S.-made clothing. The tariff, therefore, protected U.S. clothing makers, who have higher manufacturing costs than Mexican clothing makers.

---

[1] tariff: a charge added to the cost of goods brought into one country from another

4   In the same way, Mexico put a tariff on certain goods made in the United States. The tariff protected Mexican manufacturers: they can't make the same products as cheaply or as well as U.S. companies can.

5   Under NAFTA, the United States, Canada, and Mexico promised to get rid of these tariffs and other trade barriers. Factories in any of the three nations could make products and sell them anywhere from southern Mexico to northern Canada. Trade would be similar to that between, for example, New York and New Jersey. There is no import tax on goods exchanged between these states. There is no limit on what or how much can be traded, either. NAFTA would unite the three nations as one giant market of more than 360 million consumers. With so many more buyers and sellers of goods, more products would be made—and many jobs created. The treaty would increase trade, lower prices, and boost the economy of all three countries.

The Case Against NAFTA

6   The NAFTA issue caused heated debate between Democarats and Republicans. The people in the two parties disagree on most major issues. But when it came to NAFTA, many of them crossed party lines and took the same side.

7   Opponents of NAFTA focused on one point. The treaty, they said, would cost many Americans their jobs. The opponents believed that U.S. companies would move their factories to Mexico. Workers there earn much less money than those in the United States and Canada. A company could save a lot of money by paying low wages to Mexican workers. As a result, NAFTA opponents believed, many Americans would lose their jobs to Mexican workers.

8   Opponents made another point. They worried that the United States would no longer be able to govern its own affairs. For example, they feared that the rules of the treaty would weaken U.S. pollution laws. The United States has strict laws to protect the country's land, air, and water. NAFTA opponents noted that Mexico's laws against pollution are less strict than U.S. laws. Many people feared that U.S. companies would move to Mexico to avoid the demanding U.S. laws.

The Case For NAFTA

9   NAFTA supporters agreed with opponents on one point. Some low-skill jobs *would* be lost. However, the supporters argued, such jobs would be lost anyway: in time, these low-skill jobs would go to people in low-wage countries such as China. Paul Tsongas [sŏn´ gŭs], a well-known Democrat, was not worried about losing low-skill, low-wage jobs. He wrote, "I don't want to see Americans competing with Mexicans for low-wage jobs. I want to see [them] compete with Germans and Japanese for high-wage jobs." Tsongas's words pointed to yet a higher goal of NAFTA than the added jobs caused by free trade. NAFTA would increase trade between the United States, Canada, and Mexico. And such growth in business activity would, in time, lead to greater success for all three nations and a better life for their citizens.

10   Supporters said that NAFTA would create about 200,000 jobs in the United States. Free trade would result in millions of Canadian and Mexican buyers of U.S. products. So companies would hire plenty of workers to export goods and services to these countries.

11   NAFTA supporters also felt that a free-trade pact would especially help Mexico thrive. More and higher-paying jobs would raise

Mexico's standard of living.[2] A higher standard of living would make it easier to sell U.S. goods in Mexico. In this way, NAFTA would make Mexico a more attractive place to live.

12   That, in turn, might reduce the number of illegal aliens[3] who enter the United States. Many Mexicans slip across the border each year to find better jobs. If they could have good jobs in Mexico, there would be no need to leave.

The Result

13 The NAFTA debate raged for months.

New and better jobs for workers in Mexico could reduce poverty and cut down on illegal entry into the United States.

For a while, it looked as if the treaty would not pass. But in the end, Congress approved it. The vote in the House of Representatives was 234 to 200. Both Democrats and Republicans voted for the treaty. Without support from both parties, NAFTA would not have passed.

14   NAFTA is still new, so its full effect on the business world is not yet known. Although jobs have been lost, the worst fears about NAFTA have not

---

[2] standard of living: the level of comforts and luxuries enjoyed by a group of people

[3] illegal alien: a person without proper documents who sneaks into a country to live

come to pass. Industry has created new jobs, but
the greatest hopes for NAFTA have not been ful-
filled, either. A true outcome of this historic
trade pact will take about 20 years. Only then
will the long-term effect of NAFTA show
whether it was worth all the fuss.

QUESTIONS
1. What is the goal of the North American
   Free Trade Agreement?
2. Why was the political fight over NAFTA
   unusual?
3. What were the main arguments against
   NAFTA?
4. What were the main arguments in favor
   of NAFTA?
5. What is the effect of NAFTA so far?

Statues and buildings more than 2,000 years old show the glory of the ancient Mayan world.

RUINS OF A PEOPLE

Who were the Maya?
What can be learned from the ruins
they left behind?

1   It is a warm summer day. You are in Guatemala[1] [gwä tə mä´ lə]. You follow your tour guide through a thick rain forest. Tree branches form a green roof 60 feet above you. Under your feet, the path is cool and clear.

2   You watch for monkeys and snakes, but you see none. You hope there are no jaguars nearby. On your right, two brightly colored birds start up and fly into the trees above. Are they parrots? Wild turkeys?

3   The trail ends at a wide clearing. Ahead of you is a steep, four-sided hill. Vines, bushes, and trees cling to the hillsides. In places, the growth and dirt have been cleared away. There you see

---

[1] Guatemala: a small country in Central America, south of Mexico

stone steps. At the top of the steps are smooth stone walls. Suddenly you realize that this is not a hill. It is an ancient pyramid.[2]

4   Welcome to the ancient city of Tikal [tē käl´]. The Maya [mä´yə] people founded Tikal about 2,500 years ago. At one time, about 75,000 Mayan people lived in Tikal. Then, about 1,000 years ago, they left the city. Tikal lay empty for hundreds of years. The rain forest grew, covering the city.

5   In 1848, explorers found the hidden city. Archaeologists [är kē ŏl´ ə jĭsts][3] began to dig it out. Since then, they have uncovered many buildings. They have rebuilt some others. Yet the forest hides still more buildings.

Exploring the Pyramid

6   The day of your visit, Tikal is a busy place. Archeologists are at work. They remove plants and roots from buildings and plazas.[4] They brush dirt off stone carvings. They trace writing found on monuments.

7   But no one is at work on the pyramid in front of you. Your guide says you may climb its steep walls. You decide to give it a try.

---

[2] pyramid: a structure that usually has a square ground plan and triangular walls that meet in a point at the top

[3] archeologist: a scientist who studies the remains of past human life and activities

[4] plaza: a public, open-air meeting place

8   You start your climb on a wooden ladder. At the top of the ladder, dirt and plants cover the stones. You grab roots and branches to pull yourself up.

9   After a while, you reach a cleared section. You stop for a breath. Here, each stone step is more than a foot high. The steps are even, so now your climb is much more regular.

Mayans worshipped in great pyramid temples like this one at Tikal, a city of about 75,000 people and 3,000 buildings.

10   At last you reach a landing. This wide walkway runs along all four sides of the pyramid. At one point, you see a narrow metal ladder attached to the steep wall. You climb up the ladder to another landing. The pyramid still rises above you. But this landing is as high as tourists can go.

11   You look down from this high landing. Your guide and other tourists seem as small as ants. The clearing below looks tiny. Thick green forest stretches as far as you can see. From some distance, the tips of other pyramids poke through the trees.

12   Who were the Maya? Why did they build such huge buildings? Why did these people leave the city of Tikal?

The Maya

13   The first humans to settle in the Americas were hunters from Asia. The hunters crossed into Alaska. Their descendants[5] began to move south. By 12,000 B.C., some of them had reached Central America. By 2000 B.C., various groups had settled in Mexico and Central America. The Maya were one of those ancient groups.

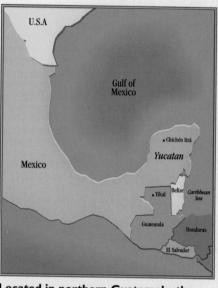

Located in northern Guatemala, the city of Tikal was founded by the Mayans about 2,500 years ago.

14   The Maya settled in the Yucatan Peninsula. Today, this land belongs to Mexico, Guatemala, Belize [bə lēz´], Honduras, and El Salvador.

15   The Maya built a great empire. By 1000 B.C., they began to form cities like Tikal. They built their first large-scale buildings. They developed a system of writing. And they became skilled in the arts and sciences.

16   By A.D. 250, Maya civilization reached its highest point. At that time, Tikal was at its best as

---

[5] descendant: a person in a later generation of the same family

well. Both that city and the rest of Maya civilization stayed strong for more than 600 years.

Maya Achievements

17　The Maya lived in ancient times, but their
achievements were vast.[6] Their architects built
massive pyramids. They built noble temples and
grand palaces. And they built everything by hand.
They had no modern machines to do the work.

18　　Maya artists were skilled at sculpture, painting,
and pottery. They depicted gods in their art. But
they also depicted common people. For example,
sculptures found in Mayan tombs show young
ballplayers and old men. They show women
weaving cloth.

19　　The Maya were highly skilled in math and
astronomy.[7] In these areas, the Maya outdid all
other peoples of the Americas. They outdid most
of the rest of the world too.

20　　The Maya number system was based on 20.
Unlike other systems of that time, the Maya
system had a figure that stood for zero. The
system could also represent very large numbers.

21　　Maya astronomers carefully observed the sky.
They studied the sun and moon, and they
watched the planets and stars that can be seen by
the naked eye. They kept track of their findings.

---

[6] vast: very large
[7] astronomy: the study of the planets and stars

From these findings, the Maya could predict the exact date and time of future eclipses.[8]

22   The Maya were also skilled at tracking days and years. In fact, their complex[9] [kŏm plĕks´] calendar was the most accurate in the world.

Maya Life

23   Most Maya were farmers. They lived on farms or in small villages. For them, a trip to the city was probably a special event. They came for market days and for religious activities.

24   Corn, or *maize* [māz], was the most important crop for the Maya. Other crops differed from area to area. Fish and game[10] varied with the land-scape as well. Some Maya land was flat, dry sea-coast. Other land was rainy, forested mountains. Some areas were rich in precious stones such as jade. Other areas had salt mines.

25   With these varied goods, trade grew. Cities like Tikal became trade centers. Each city was usually ruled by a warrior king, but little is known about the city people. Royal families and priests lived in cities. But for years, no one knew if common people lived there too. Recently, archaeologists found many private homes in Tikal. They have not yet studied these ruins.

---

[8] eclipse: a moment in which one planet or star blocks another from the Earth's view

[9] complex: not simple

[10] game: wild animals hunted for sport or food

Mayan art often depicted gods. This stone platform features one of many skillful carvings by Mayan artists.

26   The Maya did not use wheel-drawn vehicles. They had no horses, either. Instead, people carried their own trade goods from city to city. Workers dragged huge stones from quarries to building sites. Farmers did their work by hand. In battle, soldiers used hand-to-hand combat.

Maya Beliefs

27   Temples perch on top of most Maya pyramids. This placement is meaningful in Maya worship. Religion was the most important force in Maya life. The Maya believed in many gods, but the corn god was the most powerful. Other gods included the rain god, the sun god, and the moon goddess.

28   The Maya believed that blood sacrifices[11] pleased the gods. For important events, even the

---

[11] sacrifice: an offering to a god

king and queen drew their own blood. After fighting battles, the Maya honored their gods. They sacrificed some captives in front of the temple for all to see.

The End of Tikal—Almost

29 Around A.D. 900, people began to leave Tikal. No one really knows why. Perhaps trade dropped off. Perhaps bad weather ruined crops. Or perhaps the people grew angry with their king. They may have disliked the high taxes. Hard work on the pyramids may have become too much to bear.

30 The people of Tikal moved north, and the city died. For a time, Maya cities in the north grew. Chichen Itza [chē chĕn´ ē tsä´], in Mexico's Yucatan Peninsula, is an example. But within a few centuries, these cities became weak and fell to ruins too. By A.D. 1500, the Maya people had split into several states that fought each other.

31 In the next century, the empire was crushed. The Spanish invaded Mexico and Central America. They conquered the native peoples there and destroyed the active cities. They never saw the dead cities, so they never tore down the pyramids of Tikal.

32 And that is why today you too may stand where the high priests of the Maya once stood. ◆

MAYA CIVILIZATION: A TIME LINE

2000 B.C. .... Maya people settle in Mexico
and Central America.

1000 B.C. .... Maya begin to build cities,
including the city of Tikal.

0 ....Writing and calendar spread
throughout Maya region.

A.D. 250 .... Maya civilization reaches its
peak.

A.D. 900 .... Maya people begin to leave
Tikal.

A.D. 1500 .... Maya people split into several
warring states.

A.D. 1600 .... Spanish invaders crush what
remains of the Maya empire.

A.D. 1848 .... Explorers discover the ruined
city of Tikal.

QUESTIONS

1. In which modern country is the
ancient city of Tikal located?
2. When was Tikal founded?
3. List two achievements of the Maya.
4. Why are Maya temples placed so high
above the ground?
5. What happened to the Maya empire?

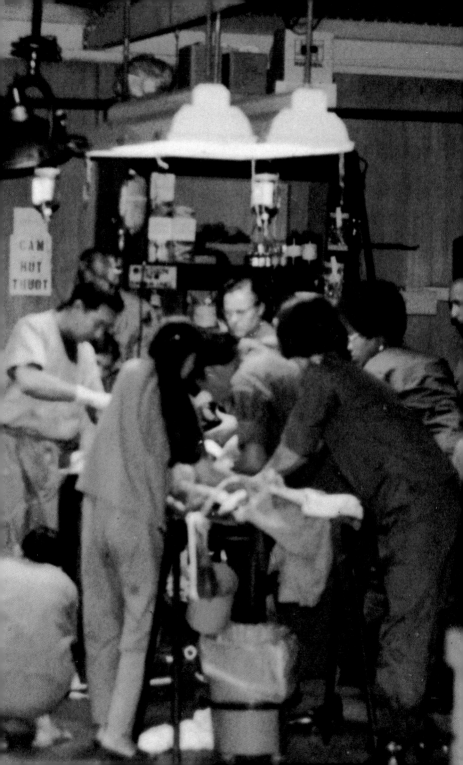

Women At **War**

*What role did women play in the Vietnam War?
How does the United States view their
contribution today?*

1 The Vietnam War was the longest war in United
States history. It was the least popular war too. It
was the only war the United States ever lost.

2 Between 1961 and 1973, more than 3.3 million
Americans served in Vietnam. More than 58,000
of them died. The names of the dead are en-
graved on the Vietnam Veterans' Memorial. This
V-shaped, black granite wall is in Washington,
D.C. People who see this memorial may be
surprised by one fact. The wall names 13
women. But in all, 65 American women died in
the Vietnam War.

Women in the Military

3 More than 7,000 military women served in
Vietnam. At that time, women did not fight in

**In this 1968 photo, United States Army nurses tend a
wounded soldier during the Vietnam War.**

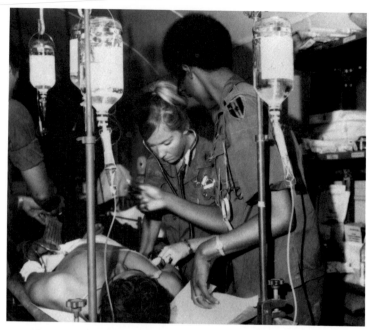

Most of the 7,000 military women who risked their lives in Vietnam were nurses. Thousands more women worked for the Red Cross, for the U.S. government, and for the press.

combat. They did not fly fighter planes. Most were nurses in MASH[1] units. These units were often in the war zone, so they were often attacked. The nurses faced danger again and again.

4   Army nurses had to deal with more than danger. They had to deal with their patients' pain and suffering. These nurses treated more than 153,000 wounded soldiers. Some soldiers were crippled for life, and many others died. As they died, the last face they saw was often the face of a nurse.

---

[1] MASH: a mobile Army surgical hospital

5   The nurses' job was heartbreaking. They treated so many men. Their patients came and went so quickly that at times, patients' faces became a blur. Nurses tried to remember each one, but they could not. Sometimes, though, one face would stand out. It might be due to the man's cries of agony.[2] It might be because of his last whispered words. Or it might be his look of fear. Years after the war, nurses still had trouble shaking these painful memories.

6   Connie Curtley was a nurse in Vietnam. Her memories of the war are painful. Her strongest memory is the smell of dirty uniforms. Curtley often had to cut these uniforms off wounded men. "I can smell that smell just like it was happening right now . . . ," she said. At times, Curtley treated so many wounded men that her own clothes became soaked in blood. "My uniform could stand up on its own almost," she said, "it was so bloody."

Civilian Volunteers

7   Thousands of civilian[3] women also volunteered to help in the war. Many of them served with the Red Cross. They brought food, medicine, and other supplies to those in need. Other women

---

[2] agony: unbearable pain
[3] civilian: a person not in the armed forces

worked for private relief groups.[4] Women also worked for the United States government and for the press.

8   These women, too, faced danger in Vietnam. Some of them died. One government worker died when the American Embassy[5] in Saigon was bombed. A mine[6] killed one female journalist. Gunfire killed another. Three missionaries[7] were killed in a hospital raid. Four women died as prisoners of war.

9   One of the worst tragedies took place on April 4, 1975. The U.S. forces had left Vietnam. A group of women had planned a mission called Operation Babylift. They feared that the children left in Vietnam would die there. So they tried to take these children out of the country to safety. Sadly, their plane crashed. Thirty-eight women and 100 children were killed.

Honoring Women Heroes

10   The Vietnam Veterans' Memorial honors 13 of the women who died in the war. But Diane Carlson Evans, a former Army nurse in Vietnam dreamed

---

[4] private relief groups: organizations, funded by private citizens, that bring aid to those in need

[5] American Embassy: the homes and offices of American officials in a foreign country

[6] mine: an explosive device hidden under land or water

[7] missionary: a person dedicated to bringing a certain religion to others

of a memorial to honor *all* of the women who
served there. Evans began planning it as early as
1983. It would take 10 years for her dream to
come true.

11   Evans formed the Vietnam Women's Memorial
Project in 1984. Workers on the project had a
great deal of work to do. They had to get
Congress to approve the idea. They also had to
design the memorial. American sculptor Glenna

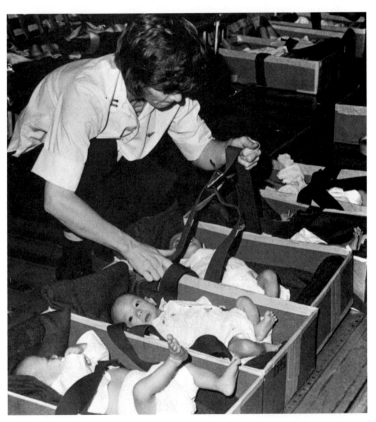

**A worker prepares infants for the ill-fated 1975 flight out of
Vietnam known as Operation Babylift.**

Diane Carlson Evans, founder of the Vietnam Women's Memorial Project, and others hug behind the newly unveiled sculpture in Washington, D.C.

Goodacre planned a stunning sculpture of four bronze figures. The sculpture features three Vietnam-era women. One of the women tends a wounded soldier.

12   Workers on the project also had to find a site for the statue. They chose a spot next to the Vietnam Veterans' Memorial. The statue would remind visitors of women's role in the war.

13   Evans's group still had to get funding for the memorial. Over the years, project workers raised

$2.5 million. Finally, the statue was built. It was unveiled on Veteran's Day, November 11, 1993. Thousands of people came to the opening ceremony. They came to thank all of the brave women who served in Vietnam.

14   For the first time in American history, a memorial to honor women's service to their country is dedicated in the nation's capital. The statue not only celebrates the women's courage and loyalty to the United States. It also reminds all people of the huge human toll that war always takes. ◆

QUESTIONS
1. When did the Vietnam War take place?
2. What role did women military nurses play in the Vietnam War?
3. In what ways did nonmilitary women serve in the war?
4. What did Diane Carlson Evans have to do to get a memorial built?
5. What does the Vietnam Women's Memorial look like? Where is it?

THE COLD FACTS

*What is fact and what is myth
about fighting the common cold?*

1   "They can send an astronaut to the moon, but they can't cure the common cold." How many times have you heard that? It's true that people have landed on the Moon. It's also true that after all these years, people on Earth still catch colds. Why can't we get rid of a common ailment that causes *30 billion* lost days of work or school each year?

Virus-Driven

2   Because a virus causes it, the common cold still has no real cure. There are about 200 different cold viruses. Sooner or later you will probably catch a cold caused by one of these viruses.

Bed rest helps you recover from a cold, but do you know how to avoid catching one?

A vaccine[1] [văk sēn´] against one kind of virus
does not stop infection[2] by another. But take
heart. There is a *sort of* cure for the common
cold: time. A cold simply needs to run its course,
which takes about a week. All you can do is get
through that week as comfortably as you can.

Telltale Signs

3   The first sign of a cold is usually a sore throat.
You can help a sore throat in three ways: by
sucking on a cough drop, using throat spray, or
gargling with warm salt water. These treatments
will ease the pain, but they won't stop a cold
from taking hold. Research shows that mouth-
wash won't help fight off a cold at all.

4   Next comes the runny, stuffy nose. This is the
body's way of fighting the virus, but you don't
have to put up with it. Using nose drops or
sprays can help stop a runny nose.
Although you may have
heard differently, using these
medicines will *not* make a
cold last longer than usual.
Just take care not to use
them for more than three
days. If you do, you may

---

[1] vaccine: a mixture containing a virus given to prevent
a disease

[2] infection: the state produced by a germ or disease

need more and more drops or spray to keep your nose clear. These medicines may also raise your blood pressure. You could try cold pills instead, although doctors say they don't work as well.

Aches and Pains

5   Fever and body aches also come with some colds. The best thing to do is rest and drink plenty of water or juice. Aspirin may help, but it is not good for children. No longer just a family cure, chicken soup seems to work wonders for a cold that also brings aches. Some doctors say the salt in the soup keeps you from drying out, which makes you feel better. Others say any hot drink or soup will do the job.

6   A cough often appears near the end of a cold. For a dry cough that keeps you awake, take simple cough syrup. A cough drop with menthol may ease a cough that tickles your throat. If your cold lasts longer than 10 days, you should call a doctor. Chances are that the cold has become a sinus or ear problem, and you'll need something stronger than cold medicines to knock it out.

The Flu

7   Influenza [ĭn flōō ĕn´ zə], or the flu, also affects your nose and throat, but it's different from the

common cold. The flu strikes fast and is more dangerous. Often hitting harder than a cold, a bout of flu will likely send you to bed for a week or so. If you get the flu, you should call a doctor. Better yet, you should see a doctor *before* you get sick. There are vaccines for the flu, which is caused by only a few different viruses.

Staying Healthy

8 The best way to beat a cold is to not catch one. It is actually harder to get a cold than you might think. When you're in good health, your body works hard to fight a virus. Eating well and getting plenty of rest and exercise are your best defenses[3] against colds.

9   Keep from catching a cold by not letting the virus enter your body. Don't get too close to someone with a cold. Spend as little time as possible in places filled with people, such as a day-care center, an elevator, and a doctor's office. Even with care, you will likely catch a cold from someone you live with. This is especially true if you live with smokers. Get out of the way when they sneeze or cough. Wash off door handles, phones, and anything else that smokers touch. Use your own towel and cup. Whatever you do, wash your hands often, and use soap. The most

---

[3] defense: a means of holding back an attack

If your job keeps you in close contact with others, it's easy to catch cold often.

common way to spread a cold is through the
hands. Don't touch your nose or eyes, or you
might pass the cold virus right into your body.

10   Vitamin C will not stop you from catching a
cold. It can, however, make it less of a problem.
Some people take lots of vitamin C at the first
sign of a cold. It may help.

Myths About Colds

11   You have probably heard that you'll catch a cold if you get a chill. An important study showed that this is not true. The study used three groups of people. One group was given nose drops that contained a cold virus. The people in this group then stood in a cold room for one half-hour wearing wet bathing suits. The second group took the same drops but did nothing else. The third group took no drops but stood in the cold room in wet bathing suits. People in the two groups that took the drops caught colds. The third group did not get sick. The chill didn't matter a bit.

12   What about the saying "Feed a cold, starve a fever"? It's not true, either. Someone with a cold or the flu may not feel like eating. There is no good reason for a person who feels that way to eat if he or she is not hungry.

13   Researchers have not given up trying to cure the common cold. Laboratories worldwide are working on a number of possible cures. Perhaps a certain vitamin can help the body fight off colds. Or, there may be a way to kill a virus after it enters the body. Maybe people who are under little stress *can* avoid catching colds better than others. Now and then you may hear that a cure for colds is just around the corner. When that rumor becomes fact, you can bet that everyone will tune in for the details! ◆

QUESTIONS

1. What causes the common cold?
2. Why should cold sufferers stop using nasal sprays or drops after three days?
3. Why is a vaccine helpful in preventing the flu but not a cold?
4. What are three ways to avoid getting a cold?

American pilot Charles Lindbergh, nicknamed Lucky Lindy, made the first non-stop flight across the Atlantic Ocean in 1927.

Flying
THE DREAM COME TRUE

Have you ever wished for a pair of wings? Will you settle for an airplane?

1   The first humans saw birds flying. At night, they saw the smoke from fires lift into the air. They watched shooting stars. Ancient people saw all of these things and wished that they too could sail across the sky. They dreamed of flying. They told stories about people flying—with their own wings, on the back of a bird, or on magic carpets.

2   Humans, however, were not built to fly. They would have to use their minds to learn how to defeat gravity.[1]

Early Ideas

3   Early people themselves could not fly or build machines that flew. So at first, they sent objects soaring through the sky. Stone Age people sent arrows through the air. People in ancient China flew kites.

---

[1] gravity: the pull on bodies toward Earth's center

4   In what is now Australia, early people first made the boomerang. This curved piece of wood is tossed into the air. It slices flat across the sky and then sweeps upward. Then it may make a circle and return close to where it started.

5   People worked for centuries on two types of aircraft: lighter than air and heavier than air. Think of smoke from a fire lifting into the air. The smoke rises because it is lighter than air. A hot-air balloon rises because the air or gas inside is lighter than air.

6   Like a bird, a craft that is heavier than air (such as an airplane) propels[2] itself through the air. It has broad wings. Air flowing over and under these wings allows the craft to lift.

7   Roger Bacon lived more than 800 years ago in England. Bacon thought that there would some-day be a machine that could fly. He had an idea for a flying machine that was heavier than air. It had wings that flapped like those of a bird. Bacon wrote, "Machines for flying can be made in which a man sits, and . . . wings strike the air in the manner of a bird." Bacon also had the idea for a balloon, a craft that is lighter than air.

8   A few hundred years later, the great artist and scientist Leonardo da Vinci [lā ə när´ dō dä vĭn´ chē] was working in Italy. In about 1490, he drew sketches of a flying machine that had a

---

[2] propels: drives forward

propeller. It took hundreds of years for Bacon's and da Vinci's ideas to become real.

Lighter-Than-Air Craft

9 In 1783, the first hot-air balloon rose into the sky. The event took place in France. The riders were a duck, a rooster, and a sheep. As the king and

In 1783, a hot-air balloon set out from Paris, France, in the first free rise from Earth to carry humans. Heated air inside the balloon expanded and made the whole craft lighter than the outside air, causing the balloon to rise.

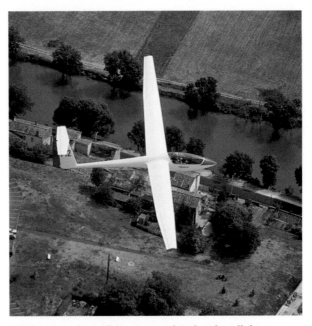

With no engine, gliders were the simplest lighter-than-air craft. Modern gliders can reach high speeds and stay in the air a long time.

his family watched, the balloon rose 6,000 feet. A month later, the first humans rose into the air in a basket under such a lighter-than-air balloon. The age of flying had begun.

10   It was not enough to have aircraft that just floated with the wind. People also wanted to steer their aircraft. That came about in 1852 when a balloon with a hard outer body lifted into the air. It was called a *dirigible* [dĭr´ə jə bəl]. A small steam engine turned a propeller. Henri [ŏn rē´] Giffard of France steered the airship with oars.

11   However, steam power was dangerous to use in balloons. So Alberto Santos-Dumont of Brazil

powered his balloon with a gasoline engine. In 1901, Santos-Dumont steered the balloon over the city of Paris for seven miles.

12   In the early 1900s, dirigibles were built in Europe and in the United States. These airships became known as *Zeppelins* [zĕp´ə lĭns]. One after another crashed, burned, or became lost. In 1937, on a trip from Germany, the famous *Hindenburg* Zeppelin exploded as it tried to land in New Jersey. There were 97 persons on board the ship. Thirty-five of them were killed. No more dirigibles were made after that tragedy.

13   An airship with a soft outer body is still made today. People know it as a *blimp*.

Heavier-Than-Air Craft

14   While some people worked with balloons, others were working on heavier-than-air craft. By the middle 1800s, people gave up the idea of flapping wings. Gliders were the first heavier-than-air machines to fly. They had wings, but the wings didn't move. A glider had no engine, either. The craft soared through the air on the force of wind beneath the wings. A book about gliders published in 1881 showed how they stayed in the air much like birds did.

15   In 1893, Lawrence Hargrave of Australia invented the box kite. It worked much like a glider, but it had two sets of flat wings. European

airplane builders made the
first biplanes[3] after
seeing Hargrave's kite.
Before long, Americans
were also making biplanes.

16   People everywhere
were interested in building
flying machines. In 1896, a
group of men set up a
camp on the sands of Lake
Michigan. They were the
first to build a flying machine with curved wings.
But their longest flight
lasted only 48 seconds.

Among the American sky
pioneers of the 1920s was Bessie
Coleman, the first African-
American female flyer.

Tests with
Powered Flight

17   Then came powered flying machines that carried
people. The first of these did little more than hop
across the ground. Some got a few feet off the
ground. Samuel P. Langley of the United States
called his large steam-powered model an *aerodrome* [âr′ ə drōm]. Langley flew the aerodrome
half a mile in 1896. The trip took a minute and a
half. With his helper, Charles M. Manly, Langley
kept trying to improve the aerodrome.

---

[3] biplane: an airplane with two sets of wings

The World's First Flight

18 Two American brothers, Wilbur and Orville
Wright discovered how to keep a plane in the air.
The Wrights had read about the flying machines
in Europe and the United States. First they made
gliders with wings that could be twisted up and
down. These wings helped to control the gliders'
side-to-side motion. Next the Wrights built a
power airplane. It had a 4-cylinder [sĭl´ ən dər],
12-horsepower gasoline engine. It also had pro-
pellers and a wingspan[4] of more than 40 feet.

19 In 1903, the Wright brothers shipped their
new machine from Ohio to Kitty Hawk, North
Carolina. That year, on December 17, Orville
Wright flew the plane 120 feet. The trip lasted 12
seconds. It was the first successful, heavier-than-
air flight that was engine-powered.

20 The Wright brothers continued to build airplanes. By 1905, they had a plane that flew 24
miles in 38 minutes. In 1908, Wilbur took a new
airplane to France to show the kings and queens
of Europe. That same year, Orville sold to the
United States government the first plane it owned.

Prizes for Progress

21 Interest in airplanes continued to grow. Flyers
won cash prizes for flights that broke new

---

[4] wingspan: the distance between the tips of an
airplane's wings

records. These pilots tried to see how fast and far their planes could go, and how long they could stay in the air. In 1909, Glenn Curtiss won a prize for flying his plane at a speed of 48 miles an hour—a world record. The next year, Curtiss won $10,000 for flying from Albany, New York, to New York City.

22   The first flight across the United States took place in 1911. Calbraith Perry Rodgers flew from Long Island, New York, to Long Beach, California. The trip took 49 days. It wasn't until 1923 that an airplane flew nonstop from New York to California.

23   In 1924, U.S. Army pilots tried to fly around the world. They flew in four planes. Only two planes finished the trip, which took more than 15 days. In 1926, Richard E. Byrd of the U.S. Navy flew over the North Pole. In 1929, he flew over the South Pole.

Crossing the Atlantic

24   Still, no one had ever flown alone across the Atlantic Ocean. No one had crossed it without stopping, either, but many people tried. In 1927, Charles A. Lindbergh achieved both of these goals in one trip. The American Pilot flew his plane, the *Spirit of St. Louis,* from New York to Paris in 33 1/2 hours. The trip made him a hero. People called him the Lone Eagle and Lucky Lindy.

25   After that event, long air trips became more common. The first commercial[5] [kə mûr´ shəl] airlines began in the 1920s and 1930s. As time went on, airplane design and performance improved.

26   Today, flying across the Atlantic Ocean takes fewer than six hours. If you can afford the fare, the *Concorde* can get you across in just three hours. You can sit in a soft seat and have dinner on the way.

27   Of course, human interest in flying did not stop at the sky. Like the shooting stars that charmed ancient people, spacecraft have gone far beyond the air around Earth. But that is another story. ◆

QUESTIONS

1. What are the two main types of aircraft?
2. What was the first lighter-than-air craft?
3. Why were dirigibles no longer made after 1937?
4. Name two kinds of heavier-than-air craft.
5. What made Charles A. Lindbergh famous?

---

[5] commercial: relating to business

The Woman
BEHIND THE LENS

*How did Dorothea Lange change history
with a picture?*

1   The year was 1913. Dorothea Lange had never
taken a photograph [fō´ tə grăf]. She had never
even held a camera. She had just finished high
school. But Lange already knew that what she
wanted out of life. She wanted to be a photographer [fō tŏg´ rə fər].

Starting from Scratch

2   Lange got to work on her dream. She needed to
learn everything about her chosen field. So she
went to work for a series[1] of photographers. She
learned something from each of them. Lange
studied under Clarence White, who taught her an

**The suffering she saw led Dorothea Lange to the streets to
photograph people in the real world.**

---

[1] series: several in a row

important lesson. Each photograph, he said, should speak for itself.

3   In 1918, Lange made plans for a trip around the world. She hoped to take photos to help pay her way. But in San Francisco [frăn sĭs´ kō], all her money was stolen. She had to give up the trip. Instead, she found a job. She saved her money and made many friends. In 1920, with the help of a friend, Lange opened her own portrait studio.[2]

4   For the next 10 years, most of the pictures Lange took were of rich people. Her skills were good, and her business was a success. But to her, something was missing. She wasn't always pleased with her work.

5   Then, in 1929, the Great Depression[3] began. Millions of people lost their jobs. Many lost their homes and farms. Whole families had little or nothing to eat. Lange saw the suffering all around her. It was hard for her to see this misery and still work among the rich. She gave up her portrait business. She took her camera out of the studio and into the real world. Lange said she would now photograph "all kinds of people."

[2] portrait studio: a work space where a photographer poses a person in special lighting

[3] Great Depression: the period of bad times and loss of money worldwide brought on by the stock market crash of 1929

Photographing the Poor

6   On her first day on the streets, Lange took a famous photo. She called it "White Angel Bread Line."[4] It shows a man waiting in line for free soup. There was no soup left. Lange captured[5] the man's look as he was turned away. He is leaning on a railing holding a cup. He looks careworn and very grim.[6] The photo shows how many people felt during the Great Depression.

7   Lange caught other images of pain and suffering. She went where poor people worked and lived. She took many photos of the awful working conditions in factories. But her specialty[7] was showing the hard life of farm workers.

8   The goal wasn't just to show that these people were poor. Lange also wanted to get inside these workers. She later said she wanted to catch "their pride, their strength, their spirit" on film.

9   One day in 1936, she passed a pea-pickers camp. She stopped to look around. Then Lange took her most famous photograph. Called "Migrant[8] [mī´ grənt] Mother," it shows a woman staring off into space. She is holding a baby on

---

[4] bread line: a line of people waiting to receive free food
[5] captured: caught in a lasting form
[6] grim: sad and stern
[7] specialty: the thing one does best
[8] migrant: moving from one region to another by chance or plan

This detail of "Migrant Mother" (1936), Lange's best known photograph, shows the misery caused by the Depression. The photo was published worldwide to raise funds for medical supplies.

her lap. Two older children bury their faces in her shoulder. The photo shows the mother's deep worry. It also shows her courage [kûr´ ĭj].

World War II

10 During World War II, Lange continued to show how some people suffered. Japanese Americans,

or Nisei [nē sā´], were born in the United States. But their parents had come from Japan. During the war, the United States and Japan were enemies.

11   Many Americans didn't trust the Nisei. Neither did President Franklin D. Roosevelt. The Nisei had broken no laws. Yet they were locked in prison camps. Roosevelt's order was a black page in American history. Dorothea Lange recorded the results on film.

Her Art Lives On

12   Lange called herself a photographer. Only toward the end of her life did she think of herself as an artist. But Lange *was* an artist long before that time. Through her camera, she was able to show the power of the human spirit.

13   In 1965 the Museum of Modern Art in New York honored Dorothea Lange. The show featuring her works was a first. No other woman photographer had ever held that honor. It is sad that Dorothea Lange died three months before the show opened.

14   The force of her work lives on. Lange's photos of the Nisei were part of a 1972 art show. People who saw these telling photos felt ashamed. One

During World War II, Lange took many pictures that showed the shameful treatment of Japanese Americans. This 1942 photo of a store owned by Japanese Americans captures the feelings of these victims of wartime prejudice.

critic wrote that the photos "convey[9] the feelings of the victims as well as the facts of the crime." ◆

---

[9] convey: to bring out; communicate

QUESTIONS

1. What was unusual about Lange's decision to become a photographer?
2. Why did Lange give up her studio work?
3. What kind of people did Lange photograph during the Great Depression?
4. How did Lange's photographs change people's feelings about the Nisei?

The great amount of cargo handled by Hong Kong's natural harbor made the small island a major center for world trade.

Hong Kong
An Uncertain Future

*Why does Hong Kong—with its impressive past—
face an uncertain future?*

1   Hong Kong is a tiny island off the southern coast
of China. This island has had an interesting past.
For centuries it was almost empty. Yet today,
nearly six million people live in the Hong Kong
area. These people face an uncertain future.

A British Colony

2   Hong Kong began as a small fishing community.
Pirates and drug smugglers also used Hong
Kong's beautiful harbor. One British leader
described Hong Kong as "a barren[1] island with
hardly a house upon it."

3   In the 1840s, China and Great Britain were at
war. Britain used Hong Kong as a naval base.

---

[1] barren: empty

After Britain won the war, it signed a treaty with China. The treaty gave Britain ownership of Hong Kong.

4   For the next century, the British used the island both as a naval base and as a trading base. Hong Kong thrived. Meanwhile, Britain added Kowloon and Stonecutters Island to its colony[2] in 1860. It later added the New Territories in 1898. Together, these areas were known as Hong Kong colony.

5   The British did not own the New Territories. Instead, they signed a 99-year lease for the area. After 99 years, Britain would have to give this region back to China.

The Colony Thrives

6   Hong Kong did well under British rule. The people were hardworking and creative in business. The economy boomed, and the future looked bright.

7   In the 1930s, Japan went to war with China. The Japanese invaded China. Hundreds of thousands of Chinese fled to Hong Kong for safety.

8   In 1939, World War II broke out. During the war, the Japanese attacked Kowloon and the New Territories. The British surrendered[3] Hong

---

[2] colony: a territory controlled by a distant nation
[3] surrender: to give up control

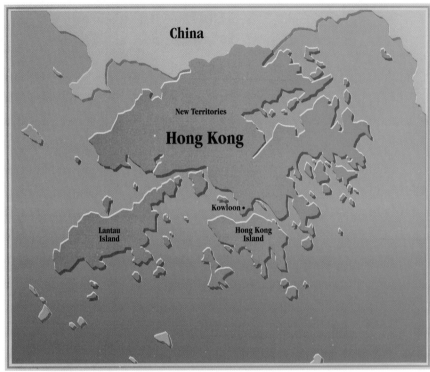

Hong Kong Island, Kowloon, and the New Territories were the main regions in eastern Asia known as Hong Kong colony, under British rule.

Kong to the Japanese. However, the Japanese lost the war in the end, and the British regained control of Hong Kong in 1945. By this time, about 600,000 people lived there.

9   After World War II, civil war[4] broke out in China. In 1949, the Communist side won this

_____

[4] civil war: a war between opposing groups in the same country

With nearly six million people, Hong Kong is one of the world's most crowded places.

war. Again, hundreds of thousands of Chinese fled to Hong Kong. They did not want to live under communism.[5] The population of Hong Kong swelled to about 2 million.

10   Immigrants continued to pour into the colony. By 1971, Hong Kong had 4 million people. By 1995, more than 5.5 million lived there. The sleepy fishing village had become a crowded, busy region.

---

[5] communism: a type of government in which the state controls the production, distribution, and price of all goods and services

Boomtown

11 Throughout the years, the immigrants turned Hong Kong into a boomtown. They worked hard for low wages. Investors sank money into Hong Kong. Its manufacturing industry grew. Its banking business grew. It developed a stable free-market economy.[6]

12 Hong Kong became a major center for world trade. The tiny colony carried on more trade than all of China. In fact, it became the eighth-largest trade center in the world.

13 Hong Kong's success made it attractive to the Chinese communists, who wanted the colony to be part of China again. They could have just taken it. The British would not have defended Hong Kong against a military attack. No one, however, wanted a war, least of all the Chinese. They wanted control of a healthy Hong Kong. Why damage the thing they wanted to possess?

An Agreement

14 In September 1984, Britain and China reached an agreement. Britain agreed to return Hong Kong to China. They named a date: July 1, 1997. This was the date when Britain's 99-year lease on the New Territories would end. But now it would

---

[6] free-market economy: a type of economy in which people or companies compete with each other as they produce and sell goods and services

be the date when Britain would hand over the
rest of the colony as well.

15   The agreement caused a problem. China was
communist, but Hong Kong had a free-market
economy. How could Hong Kong survive under
communist rule? The 1984 agreement tried to fix
this problem. The fix would last only for a set
time. For at least 50 years, Hong Kong would
keep its way of life. It would keep its legal,
social, and economic systems. The Chinese
invented a slogan for this fix. They called it
"one country—two systems."

An Uncertain Future

16 On July 1, 1997, Britain kept its part of the 1984
agreement; it gave Hong Kong colony back to
China. "One country—two systems" may not
work. China and Hong Kong have different
economic systems. In China, the government
runs the economy. People do not have much
personal wealth. In Hong Kong, people can
work hard and earn money. They live well.

17   China and Hong Kong also have different
types of government. As a British colony, Hong
Kong was not a true democracy.[7] However, its
people had a number of freedoms. They had

---

[7] democracy: a type of government in which people have
the power to elect representatives to the governing body

On a 1989 hunger strike, students in Peking, China, raise a freedom banner in Tianamen Square.

more freedom than their neighbors in China.

18   In 1995, the people of Hong Kong held an election. They elected Democrats to the legislature[8]—for a good reason. They wanted as much democracy as possible before the 1997 handover. The more Democrats in power, they thought, the harder it would be for China to take away people's freedom.

19   The Chinese frowned on the election. They said that they would close the legislature after

_____

[8] legislature: the part of a government that makes laws

the takeover. Then they would name a new legislature. The People of Hong Kong would not get to elect the new members. Instead, China would appoint them.

20   In 1996, eight Democrats from Hong Kong flew to the capital of China. They wanted to talk with China's leaders. They planned to ask them not to close the legislature. But the Chinese leaders did not want to talk. They would not even let the eight spokespersons get off the plane.

21   What does all this mean for the future of Hong Kong? The signs are not hopeful, judging from recent events in China. In 1989, the Chinese crushed a freedom movement in their own country. They did it with brutal force. In early 1997, the top Chinese leader died. His death makes the future even harder to predict. For the present, Hong Kong continues to thrive. But now that Hong Kong again belongs to China, its people wait and wonder what the future holds for them.

QUESTIONS

1. How did Great Britain come to control Hong Kong colony?
2. How did Britain's control of the New Territories differ from its control of the rest of the colony?
3. What agreement did Britain reach with China in 1984?
4. What is the meaning of the phrase, "one country—two systems"?